The Color Question In The Two Americas

Bernardo Ruiz Suarez

THE COLOR QUESTION
IN THE TWO AMERICAS

BY

DR. BERNARDO RUIZ SUAREZ

TRANSLATED BY

JOHN CROSBY GORDON

THE HUNT PUBLISHING CO.
34 WEST 136TH STREET
NEW YORK
1922

Printing Statement:

Due to the very old age and scarcity of this book,
many of the pages may be hard to read due to the
blurring of the original text, possible missing pages,
missing text, dark backgrounds and other issues
beyond our control.

Because this is such an important and rare work, we
believe it is best to reproduce this book regardless of
its original condition.

Thank you for your understanding.

DR. BERNARDO RUIZ SUAREZ

To The

Reverend Charles D. Martin, D.D.,

PASTOR OF BETH-TPHILLAH MORAVIAN CHURCH
IN NEW YORK

IN APPRECIATION OF HIS WARM FRIENDSHIP AND AS A
TRIBUTE TO HIS CULTURE AND MODESTY,
THIS BOOK IS DEDICATED.
MAY HE ACCEPT THE DEDICATION WITH A BENEVOLENCE
EQUAL TO THE SINCERITY WITH WHICH
IT IS PROFERRED.

BERNARDO RUIZ SUAREZ

TABLE OF CONTENTS.

BY WAY OF EXPLANATION.

DR. Bernardo Ruiz Suarez is not a physician. He is by profession a lawyer, and by inclination a poet. Another feature about this interesting personality which may be surprising to people who are not accustomed to referring to a lawyer as "doctor," is that what appears to be his middle name is in reality his last name, as names go in the United States. The last word of the sonorous appellation which distinguishes this doctor lawyer merely indicates that in a large number of countries where women do not vote, they nevertheless enjoy the privilege, if not the obligation, of keeping their own surnames after marriage and of transmitting them to their children. This is something that the most advanced of feminine feminists have not secured under the Nineteenth Amendment. All of which goes to show, if nothing else, that one-half of the world does not know how the other half lives.

Mr. Ruiz has come to find out and tell how the people of the United States live. Incidentally, he proposes to say something as to how the people of his native Cuba live. He has chosen for a start, a subject which affords a good basis of comparison, and in which he is particularly interested. A keen and active observer, his impressions should merit the consideration of those who, like himself, are ceaselessly engaged in the quest and utilization of knowledge.

In undertaking to express in English the ideas of Mr. Ruiz, by his request, I have been mindful of the popular tradition that a translation can never fully and faithfully represent the original work. This notion is not without some basis in fact. When, for instance, a letter in Spanish begins with the salutation *Muy senor mio y de toda mi consideracion,* and this is translated into English as "My dear Sir," "Dear Sir" or plain "Sir," to persons ignorant of one or both of these languages it is quite obvious that something has been lost in the translation.

To the readers of The Color Question In The Two Americas, I believe that I am justified in offering the assurance that whatever may have been lost in the translation from the Spanish original is, like Iago's purse, "something, nothing." Something, perhaps, has disappeared in the number and form of his words, but nothing has been altered or subtracted from the ideas of the author of this book.

THE TRANSLATOR.

FOREWORD.

I HAD always been seduced by the fantastic tales which reached my foreign ears and eyes from the pages of the book of life of the people of the United States. Ever more insinuating, ever more persuasive, that seductiveness caused me to abandon the soil of my beloved Cuba and come to this land of inconceivable potentialities, so as to get a closer view of its greatness and an intimate understanding of its defects. In the following pages I have essayed to set forth, not in the vein of a critic but rather as an apprentice and an observer, the impressions which I have received of that phase of American life with which I have been chiefly connected.

As an apprentice for "Americanization," the subject and form of this book may indicate that I have been apt, for this is not the collection of verses in which I had hoped to temper the tropical warmth of my race and my country with the soft sunshine and melancholy snow of New York. Instead of expressing subjective emotions, which could be of very limited appeal, I have directed my purpose in a more practical channel, affording at once an opportunity for self-expression and a subject of throbbing interest to the vast millions of the United States.

In presenting my impressions of the color question, I need hardly state that I have no theory to offer, with the force of dogma, for the solution or attenuation of the problems arising from the relations of the white and colored races in the United States. I am simply discussing, in the light of my experience or knowledge of the black man and his descendants in parts of Spanish America, my observations with regard to the colored man as I have seen and known him in New York. Here, I believe, is to be found the synthetic, typical colored man of the United States. Following these brief sketches of the type, I hope to offer a fuller study when I shall have observed the variants. in the Southern States especially.

THE AUTHOR.

FOREIGN OPINION REGARDING THE
AMERICAN NEGRO.

HAVING devoted myself, as a young man, to secure, with the aid of other right-thinking elements, the improvement of the condition of the colored race in my native land, I early came in contact, and have since kept in touch, through the periodical press as well as books devoted to the subject, with the development of thought and action in regard to the problems affecting the millions of black people of the United States.

In the Spanish-American countries, very little is known regarding the ability and progress of the black man of this country. In the social and political circles of colored people as such in those countries, it is a common thing to hear, as an incontrovertible postulate of racial and intellectual superiority, the statement: "I am not an American negro." This characteristic expression of contempt has the force of dogma with people who, being neither superior nor inferior to the objects of their contempt, but simply different by training and education and, to some extent, by ancestry, have made themselves the standard bearers of racial aristocracy. Nevertheless, we cannot but forgive those who think in this way, when we consider the isolation of the black man of the United States, which has given rise to the belief, among those who do not know him, that he is docile, indolent and unprogressive.

The colored people of Spanish-America are unjust, or rather mistaken, in their opinion of their Anglo-American brother. The black race in the United States has given ample evidence of its progressiveness in its churches, its theatres, its manifold efforts for economic independence, in a word in all the varied activities which, among civilized peoples, are held to be characteristic of a progressive race. But, unfortunately, I have reached the conclusion that the American negro has not a definite personality, and that such a personality cannot be distinguished clearly for many years to come, if ever, in a land of and for white people.

However, the United States is not the only country where the blacks are struggling against absorption by the overwhelming influence of the white race. Even in the vastnesses of Africa, the cradle of the black race, white men have gone in the name of a superior, civilized and civilizing race, and have enslaved peoples who were by nature free. The European spheres of influence in the heart of Africa have never represented, in my opinion, the work of humanity. I have always regarded them as manifestations of boundless egoism and love of conquest. Of course, it cannot be denied that some material progress has been made in the conquered territories and, to those who abuse the word humanity, the enslavement of weaker peoples in the name of humanity has been fully justified.

It is, therefore, not at all surprising that, in the countries conquered and colonized by and for the white race, the blacks have no fixed personality as a contributing factor in the general activities of society and are merely a negative quantity in the field of collective political rights, which are monopolized exclusively by those who consider themselves superior. Throughout history, from the days of Aristotle down to the present time, there have been groups of people who held as their exclusive patrimony the right to live the life of civilization, which they force to the extent they consider suitable, upon those whom they regard as inferior and existing only to serve and obey.

The white race is haughty and domineering everywhere. In those countries where religion,

education and other influences have softened the
hearts of men, the sentiment of brotherhood tends
to level the inequalities and barriers of race and
to give reality to that form of society which in
Political Science is called Democracy. But the
race which colonized and still forms the majority
of the people of the United States, with its his-
torical antecedents and its degrading record of
bloodshed, cannot be classified, in the opinion of an
impartial observer, as a democratic race.

With peoples, as with individuals, culture is not
in itself a sufficient measure of democracy, nor can
it serve its full purpose in civilization, except it
be accompanied with the habit of tolerance, of mutual respect, of reciprocal consideration, and at
times, even sacrifice.

Is the dominant race in the United States distinguished by the the habit of tolerance merely, not
to say sacrifice, with regard to the effectively subject race? The reply is frankly negative, isolated
manifestations to the contrary notwithstanding.
The look of disdain, the act of discourtesy, of which
the colored people are everywhere the character-
tistic objects, make it wholly unnecessary to cite
specific incidents in proof of what is already com-

mon knowledge. Nevertheless, this general disrespect of the whites is not without its positive advantages for the colored people. The latter know that they are regarded as inferior. They are not deceived. They do not have occasion to grasp the proffered hand of hypocrisy. The black people of the United States know just where they stand. They do not occupy a false position in the affairs of their country.

POSITION OF THE BLACK MAN IN THE
UNITED STATES AND IN SPANISH-
AMERICA.

IN the foregoing lines the idea is expressed that
the black man in the United States enjoys an
advantage in the rude frankness with which the
whites make him know his place in their opinion
and in their national organization. It is perhaps
opportune to explain the advantages of the situation of the black American by comparing it with
that of his fellow in other lands.

In the Spanish-American countries where there
is an appreciable colored population, these people
live in an atmosphere of apparent cordiality with
the white race. The latter, perhaps quite as
prejudiced as the American whites, but not so de-
monstrative, know how to conceal their sentiment
with the mantle of specious kindness and to throw
the same cloak of their hidden but none the less
keen prejudices over the eyes of the colored people who, with rare exceptions, are satisfied to trust
in the hypocritical fraternity of their masters.

Living in apparent racial equality, in apparent
community of principles and ideals, the black people of those countries have no aspirations other
than those of their *white brothers*. The personality which the black man might create for himself in those countries is nullified and destroyed

by the self-seeking tolerance of men of the race. Sometimes, as in Cuba, the effort to maintain an appearance of the absence of racial distinction has, through the instrumentality of colored men, been carried to the extent of absolutely prohibiting the formation, in any guise, of political parties composed of one and the same race.

Stupendous irony! Laws do not change the sentiments of peoples. Peoples have their laws changed, by pacific means, if possible, or by force, when necessary; nor can this be otherwise, for every violation of right is an invitation to violence and a symptom of revolt.

From my extended observation of the operation of the law which prohibits the formation of political parties on racial lines in Cuba, I am absolutely convinced that that law is merely a bit, cruelly applied to stifle the just demands of the black Cuban who, after sharing with his white countryman the hardships of the struggle for independence and qualifying for the symbols of capacity represented by the degrees of institutions of learning, cannot be satisfied to relegate himself to the position of the ignorant masses, devoid of ideals, and play a role inferior to that for which his culture

and the discharge of his duties as a citizen have
fitted him.

After all, it appears that the similar lack of a
definite, affirmative racial personality in the Afro-
Cuban as well as the Afro-American, is traceable
to opposite causes. In the one case, the white man
pretends to give him the hand of fellowship, as to
a brother reared in the same cradle. The American, on the other hand, regards him with haughty
disdain and considers him not at all as a man, a
black man, and a citizen, but simply as a negro, an
indefinite and indefinable thing, a beast at most.

Which of these two methods is more likely to
stimulate the progress of the black man? Facing
this dilemma, the pusillanimous and simple-mind-
ed, the partisans of half-tones, will find acceptable
the principles which govern the tolerance of the
Spanish-American whites, who set up no apparent line of distinction on account of race. But to
strong and noble spirits, to sincere and loyal men,
the methods of the Anglo-Saxon will be prefer-
able. They may be, and they frequently are,
rough and brutal and contemptuous. But they
goad the black man into a life of activity and,
consequently, a life creative of ideals which may
in time be realized.

THE INFLUENCE OF THE BLACK CLERGY IN THE DEVELOPMENT OF RACIAL PERSONALITY.

IN the preceding chapter we have discussed the absence of what we call the racial personality of the colored man, not only in Spanish America but also, and for different reasons, in the United States. In this country, however, the black man's lack of a definite group personality is not absolute, as it is in the countries to the South. The black American has no personality, and, indeed, no existence at all, in relation to the life of the white man. Wherever the two come in contact, the black man is submerged and asphyxiated. But, isolated by the white man's frank and uncompromising prejudice, the black man is obliged to put forth efforts which result in positive evidence of his collective capacity.

To the black man of Spanish-American origin, accustomed as he is to the destruction of all efforts looking toward collective progress of his race in order to preserve a simulated equality of opportunity which permits the whites to absorb and represent every cultural principle, it is most gratifying to observe the accomplishments of his congeners in the United States in the development of their own instruments of civilization.

The black man in the United States can and

does found schools for the education of the children of his race, who receive instruction from black teachers. He may build theatres, because he has artists of his own to perform in them. He may establish financial and commercial associations, because the race has business men and has money. But perhaps the most striking characteristics of the black people of the United States, in itself as well as in contrast with conditions elsewhere, is the development of a church in which members of the race minister to the spiritual needs of their fellows.

Not many months ago, the admission of a colored man from Cuba to a seminary in the Canary Islands was heralded by the press of the Island Republic as something of a sensation, and continued for several days to be the favorite theme of the newspapers. Obviously, the spiritual welfare of the colored Cuban is either neglected or entrusted to members of the white race, and these, it may be said in passing, are, for the most part, of foreign birth and sympathies. Consequently, the influence of the clergy, of one orthodox faith, in shaping the racial or even the national aspirations of the colored Cuban, is practically nil.

The black American, on the other hand, from earliest childhood frequents the temples of religion in which, no matter to what sect the faithful adhere, there is always to be noted a fervent devotion to the Author of all things. In his church, the black man tempers and invigorates his soul for the struggles of the present life. The word of the pastor gives form to the heart and mind of his followers and molds their future not only on principles of religious doctrine but, in larger measure, of civic virtue.

One who has lived a life free of religious interests, whose heart has not been touched by the song of praise and the sincere expression of piety and application to the Almighty, can hardly escape the religious influences of the United States. Whether by gradual adaptation or impelled by sentiments hitherto dormant within him, the irreligious stranger learns to appreciate the spiritual comfort necessary to mollify the shocks of fate and to give him strength for nobler and more difficult enterprises than those hitherto achieved.

A feature of the church in the United States, as contrasted with the religious organization of the Hispanic countries, is the different attitude toward education. In the latter countries, Church and School are antagonistic terms, for the one is orthodox and reactionary, while the other is liberal and progressive in form and substance. The American School, however, is the complement of the Church, and the preacher is the colaborator and often the substitute of the teacher. Not only is the secular instruction in large measure supervised and controlled by the clergy, but the institution known as the Sunday School, an immediate adjunct of the church, exerts an immeasurable influence in shaping the moral and civic as well as the religious outlook of youth.

The religion of the American is not a spiritual garment to be worn on Sunday morning only. It is carried, consciously or unconsciously, at all times. It permeates the life of the people. A simple but inspiring spectacle which impels the unaccustomed observer to ponder on the greatness of God and the smallness of mankind, is presented by American families when, on taking their seats at table before a meal, they reverently listen to the expressions of thanksgiving offered to God by a member of the party for the bounty of which they are about to partake.

The black American has, no doubt, acquired this practice from his white countrymen. But in preserving this and many other useful acquisitions despite his isolation and neglect, the black man of the United States gives evidence of the great sentimental and moral capacity of his race. To maintain and enhance these virtues is the task which the ministers of practical religion are performing with singular efficiency and with great promise for the future of the race.

DIFFERENT OUTLOOK OF THE BLACK
MAN IN CUBA AND IN THE
UNITED STATES.

BETWEEN the black Spanish-American and the black man of the United States there is a notable difference in training and aspirations. The latter has a more definite point of view toward the problems of life. He approaches them with more exact rules and with a spirit of accentuated idealism toward the realities of life, for to him there is no antithesis between the ideal and the real. The black Yankee has not the quixotism of his Spanish brother, yet he is no less gentlemanly, frank, ingenuous and sincere. In the home, under maternal tutelage, he begins to form a comprehension of the position which he occupies with regard to the white race. In the school, his ideas and sentiments receive definite shape and are directed toward horizons at once worthy and dignifying.

Living in an atmosphere of activity, he cannot but be industrious. His ideas are accompanied with action; he does not leave for tomorrow what he can do today, for he knows and appreciates the value of time and of things. Quick to assimilate, he welcomes the opportunities which the white race offers to study, to observe and to create. If it cannot now be said that there exists a distinct and characteristic culture of the black man in the United States, the time is not far distant when he will have extracted and assimilated from the white race the essential elements of a solid culture and a worthy civilization which he may call his own. The path to this ideal is already traced. All that is needed is some Messiah, who will surely come, to illumine with the constant sunshine of intelligent, courageous and self-denying leadership, the way of a people able and eager to go forward on the path of progress.

The sociology of today recognizes no inferior races, but it does admit the existence of superior environments. In this sense only, is the black race inferior to the white, and the black people of the United States, conscious of their ability, are exerting themselves to make their surroundings equal to those of the whites.

Not so the Hispanic black man. Actuated by an essentially different training, he complacently accepts all the initiatives of the white man without the slightest promptings of a creative spirit pointing the way to a future of independence for his collective personality. In Cuba, the black man who enjoys a measure of economic prosperity and occupies a position of distinction within his race. believes that he has accomplished the fullest mea-

sure of service to society when, after pursuing a
course of studies at a university, he busies himself
in politics, secures a good job, even though of less
importance than the office to which he aspires, and
finally settles down to live in the greatest possible
comfort and ease, if not in luxury.

Business enterprises are outside the range of his
vision. He is not concerned about the reform of
the legal systems which keep him in subjection.
He has no desire to inform himself about the hidden potentialities of his collective personality. He
is satisfied to trust in the ostensible friendship of
the white race. Unlike his American brother, the
black Cuban has no minister of his own color to
preach to him the practical religion of race ideals.
His teachers may be of his own color, but the racial consciousness of the black men may not be cul-
tivated in the public schools of Cuba. And so, the
colored Cuban who aspires to the self-dependence
of his race because he realizes the real attitude and
purpose of the whites, remains an impotent specta-
tor of the suppression and distortion of worthy
ideals of group distinctiveness in order to maintain
and ostentate a specious national unity.

On the other hand, the black man of the United

States is not merely allowed, but is stimulated and compelled by the outspoken prejudice of the whites, to develop a distinctive racial consciousness and pride. But, whether in the process of formation or when achieved, distinctiveness almost necessarily entails rivalry and conflict. And the excessive stimulation, external as well as internal, of the racial consciousness of the colored American, is accompanied with the ever present danger of a sudden and violent reaction. The frequent clashes between whites and blacks in various parts of this country are sufficiently indicative of the fact that the black American's characteristic patience and humility are not dictated by servile complacency. His latent spirit of revolt is merely kept in check by considerations of expediency. Unable to resist the superior strength of the whites, the black American bears the indignities and hardships inflicted upon him, with the hope and purpose of ultimately finding in them the courage and strength to enforce his claim to a fuller and fairer share of the common heritage of the people of the United States.

Despite the foregoing remarks, it is the opinion of this observer that the proper course to be pursued by the black American in his struggle to achieve a position in the national entity more in keeping with his capacity for progress, lies in peaceful evolution. This is a slow process, but it is constant and sure. The relentless effort toward progress, under the inspiration of competent leaders, will continue to be, as it now is, far more effective than any outbreak of violence. Revolution would be suicidal for the black people of the United States. Peaceful and patient evolution is the formula for the salvation of a race which is eager to live. Undue haste and violence must almost certainly lead to retrogression and destruction, as will be illustrated in the following pages from the history of the colored people of Cuba.

FROM POLITICS TO REVOLUTION.

U NDER the name of the Independent Colored
Political Party and in accordance with Cuban legislation covering the formation of such associations, Evaristo Estenoz, an officer of the Army of Liberation, founded the organization under discussion, in the city of Havana, in 1909. Then, as now, the colored people of Cuba were not adequately represented in governmental affairs. While it is true that there were two or three colored members of the House of Representatives, they had been nominated only as a tardy and ineffectual means of appeasing the growing discontent of the colored people.

At this juncture Estenoz, a man of courage, of industry and of civic virtue, if not of brilliant intellect, undertook the difficult task of organizing the political forces of the black people. At times violent in the language of his initial campaign, but always liberal in his ideas, he sounded a note of alarm to the conscience of the whites. Feigning indifference to the growing intensity of the efforts of the black leader, they quietly prepared to defend themselves against an imaginary attack. Despite the opinion of so distinguished a critic as Professor Fernando Ortiz, of the Law School of Havana University, the campaign of Estenoz was not

a campaign of incitement to violence against the
life and property of the whites. In the judgment
of all impartial observers, it was merely an effort
of a group of people to obtain, through the peaceful activities of a political organization, a fuller
participation in the public life of their country
and a greater measure of respect and consideration
from those with whom they had shared the trials
and sacrifices of the struggle for common independence and equality of opportunity to serve the common weal.

At first the government, under the presidency
of General Jose Miguel Gomez, appeared to lend
its moral support to the just demands of the party
of Estenoz, and this apparent sympathy of the authorities gave additional impetus to the movement.
The colored people began to see, in a not distant
future, the triumph of their aspirations for equality in fact as well as in the theory of the law.
Beautiful dream, which was shortly to be inter-
rupted by a rude awakening. The government,
which had winked at the formation of a political
force which it might be able to use to its own advantage, soon began to realize that that force was
becoming too great to be exploited and controlled
from without. It must be suppressed, and without

delay. So, in April, 1910, the leaders of the Independent Colored Party were arrested on the charge of conspiracy to rebellion, and incarcerated for several months. Finally, it was clearly established that there had been no conspiracy against the safety of the state or the stability of the government, and the courts provisionally dismissed the indictments and ordered the liberation of the prisoners.

Far from discouraging them, the temporary sacrifice of their liberty only served to stimulate the leaders of the Colored Party to continue the struggle. The movement soon received the support of the overwhelming majority of the colored people throughout the country. Pressed by the public opinion of the white population which saw in the movement of Estenoz not a simple vindication of the natural rights of a despoiled people, but an assault upon the traditional prerogatives of white supremacy by divine right, the government secured the enactment of a law which ended the lawful existence of the Independent Colored Party.

The author of this law was a colored man, Martin Morua Delgado, a man of uncommon erudition and enlightenment with regard to everything except the political interests and aspirations of his race. He was at that time President of the Senate, representing in that body the Province of Havana, and had been Minister of Agriculture.

It is difficult to justify, in the light of clear reason, the action of Morua Delgado. Those who think superficially and are carried away with high-sounding phrases will say that Morua considered himself as a citizen of Cuba and not as a black man. But those who look beneath the surface in the penetrating quest of truth will say that that otherwise brilliant man was so blinded by selfishness that he could not see that while he could live as a citizen, thousands of his brothers lived as pariahs; or he feared the prospect of the ascendancy of the leader of the Independent Colored Party and was willing to endanger the future of his race in order to maintain his own position against the growing power and influence of another man of color.

But, whatever may have been the motives of Senator Morua in introducing and sponsoring a bill which prohibited the formation of political parties composed exclusively of avowed members of one race, the fact is that, once in force, this law

furnished the spark that inflamed the Independent
Colored Party to a disastrous revolution. Martin
Morua Delgado, as a colored man, never should
have been the author of such a law. It would have
come sooner or later, but the idea and its execu-
tion should have been left to be conceived by white
members of the Congress.

The Morua Law, a denial of the right of association inherent in all free human beings, was natural-
ly and inevitably answered by a last, but rather
premature, resort to arms. In 1912, the leaders
of the prohibited Independent Colored Party gath-
ered their followers for an armed protest which
was heralded throughout the Island and abroad as a
general uprising of the black Cubans against the
white population. But the Independent Colored
Party, it may be solemnly affirmed, never contem-
plated a rebellion against the white people. The
Party and its adherents rebelled only and exclusively against the Morua Law, which had destroyed a
political organization devoted to peaceful and just
objectives.

With the revolution in progress, it was inevitable
that the white people, within and without the country, should form an opinion adverse to the causes
which had provoked the uprising and against the

black men who had dared to protest against the political servitude to which they were subjected. All the bitterness, all the hatred, all the ancestral prejudices of the white race against the black, were let loose. While the machine guns of the government troops were mowing down thousands of colored men, not alone those in arms, but the peaceful inhabitants of towns and villages in the Eastern Province of Cuba, in the larger cities and even in the Capital of the Republic, white men armed to the teeth went about ordering any and every black man to withdraw from the streets and public places on pain of death, and the mere color of his skin was sufficient reason to send a man to prison on the charge of rebellion.

The number of colored men who perished in the shortlived and unhappy revolution of 1912 is estimated at five thousand. Among them was the leader, Estenoz, who, having responded to an invitation to confer with the forces of the government on the terms of surrender and the restoration of order, was subjected to the penalty of the *Ley de Fuga*, or Law of Flight, which is a favorite euphemism for the assassination of a captured revolutionist in Latin America. His fate was shared by his associate, Ivonnet, a former officer of the

regular army of the Republic of Cuba and a
soldier whose achievements on the field of battle
had won him the rank of a general of the Army
of Liberation. These men made the supreme sacrifice in defense of the ideals and interests of their
race. If there was a touch of egoism in them, as
in all men, it was overshadowed by their largeness
of heart. And, as martyrs to their principles, they
have found consolation for their martyrdom.

THE LESSON OF REVOLUTION.

THEIR abortive revolutionary enterprise having been rapidly suffocated in blood and fire, the surviving participants in the movement were rounded up and, after summary trials before the ordinary courts, were sentenced to various terms of imprisonment. After some months the government, impelled perhaps rather by political expediency than by motives of generosity and forgiveness, secured the passage of a Law of Amnesty, which enabled the erstwhile warriors to return to the peace of their homes.

But while a general amnesty nullifies the penalty for acts which have been adjudged as criminal and may even void the juridical basis of the criminal charge, it cannot remove from men's minds the memory of past events. So the amnesty granted to the black revolutionists of Cuba in 1912 was not and could not be so general in its effect as to blot out the resentment of the white people against the rebels and their color. On the contrary, the utter failure of the movement, far from inspiring the white masses with the sense of charity and commiseration for the weak, which is characteristic of moral strength, only served as an incentive to the frank expression of the half-suppressed animosity which had given rise to the revolution.

Then began for the black Cubans a new period of trials and privation. Soldiers who had fought loyally under the banner of the Republic in the late revolution were expelled from the army. Public officials, even in the most humble capacity, were removed from their positions because of their color. Those who had not been exterminated by shot and shell were apparently to be annihilated by hunger. The rewards which the race had achieved for their devotion to the common cause of the National Independence and in recognition of the capacity of individuals, were lost in the attempt to increase those rewards by force.

The black people of the United States have far more ground for discontent and complaint than had the leaders of the Cuban revolution of 1912. These were citizens dissatisfied with their apportioned lot in the management of the affairs of the nation. The black American, generally and practically speaking, is not even a citizen of his country. He does not enjoy the ordinary rights and privileges accorded by law to citizens, and effectively enjoyed by them, provided they be white,

The black American cannot always convert into songs of mirth the strains of anguish that come swelling from the heartstrings of an outraged people. Sometimes a different note is struck, virile and resonant, revealing the grim determination of a beast, perhaps, but a beast at bay:

> "If we must die, let it not be like hogs,
> "Hunted and penned in an inglorious spot....
> "If we must die—oh, let us nobly die,
> "So that our precious blood may not be shed
> "In vain; then even the monsters we defy
> "Shall be constrained to honor us though dead." ·
>
> —CLAUDE MCKAY

This is not the language of beasts. It is the speech of a people who must not die and who need not die, least of all by suicide. The black American cannot afford to risk on a throw of the dice the success which he has achieved an the conquests which the future will open to him through his assimilative capacity. Patience, plodding and peace must be the watchwords of a people who can prove their fitness to survive only by surviving.

A POLITICAL LACUNA IN THE UNITED STATES.

IF in countries like Cuba the existence of the black race as a unit distinct from the white race is impossible because of prohibitory laws, the United States, on the other hand, offer a splendid field for the beneficient action of the black people as a distinct collectivity, because the laws and customs of this country, far from inhibiting the separatist aspirations of the colored population, tend to promote them. A proper appreciation of these circumstances should disclose to the colored people opportunities which they have apparently failed to utilize for the advantage of the race.

In the district of Harlem, for instance, which comprises most of the large colored population of New York City, there is no political party composed of members of the race. Such a party, properly organized and efficiently directed, could exert an appreciable influence in the interest of the race by throwing its strength, at the opportune moment, to one or other of the dominant parties. Such co-operation does not imply permanent attachment or fusion, which would be tantamount to dissolution. A virile political party, composed of colored citizens, would lend its support, on occasions such as electoral contests, only to the party which gave the greatest assurance of specific advantages for the race.

With a strong party, independent in its organization and control, but co-operating to mutual advantage with the dominant parties, the colored people of the United States would be a very much more weighty factor in politics than they are at present. Indeed, it is difficult to understand why such a party, working in the interest of the race, has not been organized. This anomaly cannot be attributed to the hatred and prejudice of the whites, because they themselves have insisted on absolute separation as the basic principle of their relations with the black race, and it cannot be presumed that they would oppose the application of this principle to the field of politics, while enforcing it in all the other activities of life which are inextricably associated with the political rights and duties of free citizens. Nor is it to be feared that, in order to prevent the colored population from intelligently exercising their political rights for the collective well being and not for selfish, individual advantage, the white people would assume the responsibility before civilization for the dire consequences of an ultimate appeal to force.

In the United States, the ground is fully pre-

pared for the establishment of a political party
comprising and representing the colored citizens.
First of all, there is among these people an unde-
niable spirit of association; secondly, there are millions of potential members of such an organization; thirdly, the isolation and non-interference of
the white race with regard to the colored race at
once justify and facilitate the formation of a colored party.   The absence of a colored political
party is not due to a lack of intelligence to con-
ceive, capacity to organize, ability to direct, will-
ingness to co-operate.   All these requisites are to
be found in plenty among black Americans.   The
only thing needful is the will.   Once this is creat-
ed, it will rapidly be converted into action.

There is nothing Utopian, nothing chimerical, in
the ideas here expressed.   Twenty years ago, ten
years ago, the black people of the United States
did not dream of living as they do today.   It is
their duty to better the present conditions, even as
these are an improvement on the conditions of a
decade ago.   It is criminal to remain stationary
when it is possible to go ahead.   The waters of the
sea are wholesome because of the constant flux and
reflux of the waves; but the waters of motionless

lakes are deadly because their stagnation affords life only to inferior organisms.

The black people, not alone of the United States, but of the whole civilized world, must act like the waves of the sea. They must be constantly in motion, even though a forward movement may ultimately spend itself against obstacles and be dissipated returning to its source. They must constantly renovate their ideals, their customs, their modes of action. Otherwise, they may not perish as a race, but they will be useless as a factor in civilization.

AN ASSOCIATION NEGATIVE IN ITS
PURPOSES AND RESULTS.

I N the preceding chapter we have discussed the need of a national organization of the colored people for the recognition of the race as an element of strength and usefulness within the territory of the Union. Black Americans have fully sensed and have sought to satisfy this need, but their organized efforts have been generally misdirected and totally ineffective. Especially is this true of an association of black people who aspire to bring about the wholesale migration of the race to Africa.

The impelling idea of the partisans of this movement, while it does not find the support of the general mass of colored population, certainly arouses their comment; and comment, whether with regard to the activities of peoples or the life of individuals, is always the consequence of some interest. The African migration scheme and its associated ideas constitute an important feature of the group interests of black Americans and, as such, are worthy of consideration wholly without regard to the mental capacity of the leaders of this movement.

What is the ultimate purpose of an organization ostensibly comprising the black race throughout the world, whose immediate object is to promote the reunion of the race on African soil? We are told that this gathering will create a civilized African State able to make itself felt as a power among the nations. But, for the realization of this purpose, it is surely not necessary for all black people to go to Africa, carried away with the assumption that that continent is our geographic fatherland.

The concept of nationality is based not so much on geographical boundaries as on sentiments of association, of community of interest, sentiments of far greater weight in the mind of the individual than the laws governing the acquisition of a new citizenship. Assuming that the go-to-Africa movement succeeded and that millions of civilized black people went and hoisted on that continent the flag of a new nation, their mission would have been purely speculative but at best one of conquest and dominion over the native population.

It is reasonably certain that no black man born and bred on this side of the Atlantic knows what it is to feel genuinely African, and it is doubtful whether any black alien has even a superficial sense of a common nationality with the African. The black people of the American countries, in so

far as they have sought to inform themselves on
the subject, know no more about Africa than what
they have learned from the limited contents of
text-books on geography and history. The line of
ancestry connecting them with the African natives has long since disappeared, without leaving
traces sufficient to re-establish a nexus of positive
co-relation. The descendants of expatriated Africans might live in Africa, as they live in their re-
spective countries, sometimes feeling that they are
black. But they would not be Africans.

The hypothetical African State, uniting the natives and their congeners from overseas in one common nationality, would lack the very bond of moral
identity on which such a union is predicated. But
aside from the effective absence of its imaginary moral basis, would the conjectural African
State possess the physical means to maintain itself
of and for black people. Is population the only
factor in the maintenance of a nation? The alien
element would not constitute the economic factor in
our all-black Africa State, for the black race, in or
outside of Africa, is not even moderately well off.
Without money and the ability to use it properly,
the existence of a nation, duly constituted according to form, is extremely precarious and is inevit-

ably terminated by absorption, formal or effective, by some richer nation.

The recognition of an African nation of extraneous conception and artificial foundation, would be merely conventional and subject to the conditions usually imposed on a State regarded as inferior. And our African nation would be worse than backward. It would be a backless nation. It would not rest on the secure foundation of a civilization and a culture peculiar to its people. There are civilized black people; there are cultured black men, who have absorbed the civilization of the white race and who may impart to their own race the culture and civilization which they have acquired. But these men are not sufficient in number and influence to mould a characteristic, definite African culture with elements derived from a civilization not of African origin.

The time has certainly come for the black man, wherever he may be, to enforce his claim for equality of opportunity with other men and to secure full recognition of the extent to which he has used such opportunity in the work of civilization. If the black people of one country can find inspiration and encouragement in the fact that their fellows throughout the world are engaged in the effort to improve their condition where they are, an international association may have some educational value in acquainting one group with the failures or successes of the others. Such an association, however, not only loses its usefulness, but becomes a dangerous and destructive element among the black people when it invites them to abandon their achievements, their aspirations and their labor in the land of their birth and take passage to Africa as to some terrestrial paradise where black men toil not nor spin, but wear gorgeous robes.

A NATION WITHIN A NATION.

I LLUSTRATIVE at once of the real influence of the go-to-Africa movement and of the black people's ability to appreciate and tolerate good, high-priced humor, is the fact that no enthusiastic migrant, traveling at his own expense, has got anywhere nearer to Africa than the one hundred and thirty-fifth highway running straight east and west in New York. Along this route, some few are said to be awaiting passage. One or two have crossed the Atlantic Ocean at the expense of the crowd, but they lost no time in recrossing to bring back the news that blackwater fever is no respecter of black persons born outside of West Africa. And this is about as much as the go-to-Africa association is likely to accomplish for the creation of an enduring nation of black people, respected and recognized by all civilization. So far as black Americans are concerned, their nation is within the boundaries of the United States. If they must be independent, they must find a sphere for the exercise of their independence within the Union, for they are not going elsewhere.

A Black Nation within a White Nation would perhaps be the formula for a satisfactory solution of the race problem in the United States. It would meet the demand of a majority of the whites for

the elimination of the black man from the social
and political activities of the dominant race. At
the same time, the black man would have the opportunity to develop his own political and governmental institutions without imperiling his progress
by absolutely isolating himself from contact with
the whites. In his present stage of development,
no matter what obstacles he may encounter, the
black man cannot afford to deny himself the opportunity of at least observing the ways of the white
man so as to adapt some of them to his needs. A
nation in Africa, embracing the black peoples,
would indicate the inability of the race to strive
and survive in the midst of white civilization. It
would mean the loss of three or four centuries of
effort and of achievement in human progress. On
the other hand, a Black Nation within a White
Nation would have a fair prospect not only of con-
serving its gains, but of rapidly increasing them,
once freed from the encumbrances of race
prejudice.

The ideal country for carrying out an experi-
ment of this kind is the United States. Here may
be found, in the districts occupied by colored people in the cities and other centers of population,
miniature nations in all but their political and

juridical aspects. In all else, in all those activities on which the law and politics depend, these communities of colored people are distinct from the surrounding aggregations of white people. Reassembled in some territory of sufficient extent, all or most of these miniature nations of colored people would constitute an important Black Nation within a White Nation, and its establishment would be justified if it could be accomplished by peaceful means and with the mutual consent of both groups.

The nation within a nation has long been recognized in the white man's International Law. European settlements in Chinese cities, in Turkey and elsewhere in Asia, have for generations been independent, in every practical sense, of the local and national authority. In much the same way, the Canal Zone, in the heart of the Republic of Panama, is entirely free, so far as the authority of the Isthmian Republic is concerned. The United States pays rent for the occupancy of the Canal Zone, thereby acquiring the right to fortify this territory against its Panamanian owners.

The ultimate formula for the definite constitution of a Black Nation within the United States is of secondary importance as compared with the fact

that such a nation is recognized in principle by
almost all the people of the country. The entry of
black people into a residential district occupied by
whites is followed, sometimes slowly but always
surely, by the withdrawal of the latter, who regard
as unholy the ground on which niggers tread.
There is never any question as to the impossibility
of members of the two races occupying the same
building, the same street, the same section of the
city. No matter how much they would like to remain, the whites must abandon their homes to the
blacks, as it would be harder even to kill them off
than to live near them.

Racial antagonism in the United States may not
be, in a true sense, instinctive and natural, but
custom and public opinion have made it rather
more than second nature. There is no disposition
to change the present frame of the national mind,
which asserts that fundamental, inescapable differ-
ences compel the white man to flee before the black
man whenever possible. A Black Nation within
the United States would be distinguished not only
by the color of its inhabitants, but, in all probabil-
ity, by its creation with instruments of peace and
without bloodshed. The essential weapons for such

an enterprise would be, in the phrase of Napoleon, money, money and more money. Next in importance and value would be the disposition on the part of the colored people to make the best possible use of a situation which they cannot change, as they have done in the district of Harlem, in New York.

A CITY WITHIN A CITY.

TO white New York, no less than to foreigners of more distant origin, Harlem is reputed to be a good place to keep away from. For Harlem is the name of the most compact and most thickly populated settlement of black people in the world. This fact alone would be sufficient to make the rest of New York quite foreign to Harlem. But, as the world now thinks, a city of black people must inevitably be a city of black deeds. So the fame of New York's colored city has gone abroad, and it is by no means an enviable fame.

An examination of police records would probably show that there is no greater percentage of crimes and criminals in the colored district of New York than in any similar section of the American metropolis. It may possibly be shown that there is less crime in black New York than in some other sections of the city, inhabited by peoples of the same general economic and intellectual plane, but of a lower degree of pigmentation. But what is certain is that newspaper reports of the unusual doings of malefactors can give no idea of the usual doings of more than one hundred thousand law-abiding and industrious colored residents grouped in one section of the city of New York. To know black New York, even superficially, it is necessary to live in it and observe it with an unprejudiced eye.

To the stranger expecting to find the typical kennels of the underdog, such as the hovels of the poor which disgrace many a European city, the native quarters in South Africa, or the old Chinatown in Havana, the colored section of New York is an agreeable revelation. Externally, it is far more attractive than some of the other parts of the city. Streets as clean as any are lined with buildings newer and better constructed than the flats and apartment houses in many other sections of the city. Private houses compare favorably with homes in some of the exclusive residential districts. In many instances, the interior may show evidence of a lack of adequate economic and cultural preparation of the occupants. There is some crowding and discomfort in the flats and apartments. But many of these, as well as some of the private residences, are furnished and maintained with a luxury indicative of economic ease and of a thorough appreciation of the fine art of living. And, withal, if one may judge by the manifestations of cordiality between uniformed policemen and citizens of this district, black Harlem is a

calm spot in a city frequently disturbed by crime
waves.

Most of black New York goes out of its residential limits to work for white New York.   But
enough remains at home, in Harlem, to constitute an Association of Trade, which comprises the
business and professional men of the community.
Wholesome social and moral influences are exerted
by the churches, the Y. M. C. A. and Y. W. C. A.,
as well equipped and as efficiently managed as the
branches for white people, and numerous institutions and clubs.   A public library in the heart of
the district is not merely a well patronized book-
lending institution, but through the booklovers'
clubs and other organizations which meet there, it
is an active center for intellectual inspiration.

Some time ago there was held in this library an
exhibition of the work of colored artists and wri-
ters. Among the many admirable paintings was a
canvas representing Christ washing the feet of the
disciples, which, it is said, was awarded a first prize
in the Paris Salon.   One section of the exhibition
was devoted to embroidery; another to African
handicraft, showing cloths, iron implements and
other useful objects produced by the natives.   The

book section contained thousands of volumes, in various languages, patiently collected by two colored gentlemen whose hobby is to gather from all parts of the world books written by or relating to members of their race, and whose modesty forbids the disclosure of their names, for fear that they may receive the unsought recognition of their unique service to the cause of human understanding.

It is said that this exhibition will be held annually. In time it may be held permanently. This and similar efforts, in all lines of activity, are typical of the better elements among the colored people of Harlem. And the better are far more numerous than the worse. What these people are doing in New York, they can do and are doing, sometimes with even greater success, in other cities. If they enjoyed everywhere the same freedom from interference, the same guaranties of life and property, the same opportunities to utilize for their own development the educational facilities afforded to all other elements in the community, as they do in New York, the colored people of the United States would do their full share of the work of civilization, whether the City within a City reached its logical conclusion in the Nation within a Nation, or by its sheer merits disproved the need for its existence.

THE VIRTUE AND THE VICE OF
DEMOCRACY.

OF the many hopeful aspects of the color question in the United States, not the least striking is the absence of a visible color line within the Afro-American group itself. Democracy, balked and thwarted in every attempt to exert its leveling influence against the rigid barrier between the white race and the colored, finds a generous measure of compensation in the success of its onslaughts against the strongholds of lineage and complexion in one group and the other. The color question in the United States, difficult of solution, cruel and reactionary as it is in so many of its manifestations, nevertheless represents a long step in the progress of civilization. For, after all, there is only one color question in the United States, whereas there might be two or three or half a dozen, each as troublesome as the others put together.

The colored population of this country is a social unit, not only in the broader sense of community life, but in the more intimate relations of man to man. Between the American of the color of ebony and the perfectly white man of African descent, there is nothing to suggest that the former considers himself superior because of the purity of his African blood, nor that the latter finds superiority in the scanty pigmentation of his skin. One word is used to describe these extremes and the intermediate types of this kaleidoscopic people. The other Americans, of pure European descent, are so blinded by prejudice that they only see black when contemplating their fellow citizens of African descent. The latter, with their characteristic adaptiveness, readily suppress the claims, though the evidence cannot be suppressed, of a composite and extremely varied ethnic origin. Striving and looking forward to the recognition of the oneness of the human race, they do not turn back to re-establish original lines of cleavage.

Not only by the orthodox whites, but also by the orthodox blacks, some of the mixed people are often accused of what is regarded as the heinous crime of "trying to get away from their race" or of "passing for white." As a matter of fact, it is surprising how few of those who, by every physical standard ought to be classed as "white people," do avail themselves of the opportunity of severing their connection with the despised black race. Racial distinction in the United States, rigid as it is when visible and real, does not require that citizens be labeled in order to give them a classification which nature did not establish. Custom forbids the contact of "white" people with "colored" peo-

ple in intimate social relationship. But no one has
any moral obligation to deny himself the opportunity afforded by his physical and mental qualities to
earn an honest living, because of any false sense
of respect for friends or pride of ancestry. However, most of those Afro-Americans who might be
altogether "white" prefer to be "colored" people
and some of them seem to enjoy being negroes.
But there can be no doubt that the sacrifice is often
more apparent than real, for not a little of what
passes for greatness among the weak would be
recognized as mediocrity among the strong.

Democracy, the ideal for the attainment of
which the soul of mankind is constantly striving,
like all virtues is subject to conversion into vice.
The Afro-American has established in his own
realm the equality of men without regard to their
external inequalities. It is but human that equality of physical manhood should be mistaken for
equality in things spiritual and intellectual. In a
thorough-going democracy everybody must be an
aristocrat. White America is not such a democracy, either in itself or in relation to other peoples
and especially to black America. If it were, it
could not occupy the place that it now holds with
good title, despite its many and grave defects, in

the forefront of civilization. Afro-American democracy is thorough-going; too much so for its own good.

Where everybody thinks himself the equal of anybody else, nobody is willing to be guided by the counsels of another. In such a community, there can be no leader, because there are no followers. There can be no efficient organization for the general good, for every organizer must be inspired and dominated by essentially selfish aims. Worthwhile ideas there may be, but the duplication of effort in realizing them must inevitably lead to a lessening or destruction of the effect. The Afro-American, fighting against color and caste discrimination from without, cannot afford to give it a place in his own mind and in his own conduct. But if he would remove it from the mind and heart of others, he must recognize his own individual limitations. He must suppress the envy and jealousy which impel him at all times and in all lines of activity, to attempt to do what his fellow may better do and to rejoice in bringing about the common failure rather than tolerate the possibility of another's success.

Intense individualism is the dominant note of the American character, but it is too intensely exaggerated in the character of the black American, of whatever shade he may be. Virtuous democracy calls for the self-assertion of the individual in the interest and not to the detriment of the common good. Democracy is vicious and dangerous when it is so zealous for its own conservation that it destroys the power of men to appreciate and utilize the special and distinct, if not superior, aptitudes of their neighbors. Afro-American democracy is at once a virtue and a vice in variable quantities. On the establishment of a rational proportion depends the progress of the race.

RULING BY DIVIDING.

IN contrast with the sentiment of group unity among North Americans of African blood, this ethnic strain does not constitute a unified people in the Latin American countries, least of all in Cuba. Between the pure blacks, the brown mulattoes and the yellow-white quadroons, there exist almost impassable social barriers. The black man regards the man of mixed African and European blood as a natural enemy, while the mixed man looked upon his black half-brother in much the same way as Anglo-Saxon society regards the so-called natural child, with the difference that, for the Cuban mulatto, the black brother is altogether unnatural.

Of course, there could be no rule without exceptions. The barriers are sometimes removed, not only in the ordinary relations of individuals, but by marriage. And then, if the children happen, as is likely, to vary greatly in color, they establish their social connections accordingly. It is a matter of fact that in a Cuban family, consisting of black children by a first mariage and mulattoes by a second marriage of the same mother, the difference of color made it impossible for members of both broods to attend a social function together. Especially in Santiago de Cuba, the blacks, the mulattoes and the quadroons have their separate clubs and social institutions, and they do not exchange invitations.

This exclusiveness, it must be noted, by no means implies the existence among Afro-Cubans of an instinctive and inexorable caste system which might be interpreted as justifying and strengthening the Anglo-American laws, written and unwritten, on racial distinction. The hierarchy of color in Cuba was established as a part of Spanish colonial policy. The aristocratic landowners did, perhaps, adopt a more humane and natural attitude towards their children by enslaved mothers than did the planters of the southern United States. But the consequent differentiation between the partly and the wholly black people of Cuba was further stimulated as a means of continuing their exploitation for the safety and profit of the common master. With the development of the struggle for independence, the Spanish government saw to it that grandee and commoner, white and black and yellow and brown, were kept as far apart as possible. But most of them got together on the side of Free Cuba. And Cuba believes that the surest way to maintain her freedom is to have three or four color questions which neutralize each other.

Pride of kind is a very estimable quality in
itself and for those who possess it, but its practical
value, in relation to others, depends upon the nu-
merical and economic strength of those who share
the same pride of class or race. In Cuba, the
white people outnumber all others and are even
disproportionately strong in wealth and education,
while the pure blacks are lowest in numbers and
in influence. They may feel as proud as the whites
of their purity of race and color, but they cannot
escape the cumulative effect of the pride and prejudice of all the other elements of the population.
They cannot fail to be impressed with the utter
hopelessness of attempting to rise, with their color,
above the position which tradition accords them in
the community. In common with the mixed people, they must believe that successful achievement
in the work of civilization is conditioned upon the
possession of a more or less white skin. In Cuba
the black man may comfort himself with pride in
his color. But so long as everybody else believes
that the black color is a disgrace and an evidence
of mental incapacity, there can be little effort, and
that doomed to failure, for the development of a
racial pride based on the useful accomplishments
of men of African blood.

The black people of Cuba were separated from their blood brothers of lighter hue in order that Spain might rule. Tradition maintains that division in order to facilitate and ensure the rule of the white people. But there is no danger that a white majority greater than that of South Carolina and others of the United States would cease to rule in Cuba if the mulattoes and the blacks developed a spirit of mutual respect and tolerance which would enable them to co-operate effectively for their common welfare and, therefore, for the advantage of all the people of the Island Republic.

No matter how much "white" blood they may have in their veins, the mixed people are not regarded as of the white race. No matter how little "black" blood they may have, it is an element which they have in common with the black people. In the strictly physical sense of the word, the partly white cannot be of the same race as the wholly black. But they can form and ought to form a racial unit for the development and maintenance of a self-sustaining civilization able to command from others the respect which it should accord to itself.

THE CHANGING ORDER IN CUBA.

DESPITE the persistence of the traditional distinction between the various types of mulattoes and the pure black people of Cuba, there is a marked tendency among the representative elements of all these divergent groups to get into closer contact for the promotion of their common welfare.

Following the ill-fated revolution of Estenoz, the various sections of the colored race began to perceive that they could not expect to mitigate the prejudice and discrimination which they suffered alike from the whites, while they continued to practice the same evils among themselves. Especially in the smaller towns and villages, where the scantier the colored population the keener were the lines of caste which separated them, the blacks and the mulattoes have come to associate more freely, not alone for the pursuit of objects which they recognize as of their common interest, but also in the more intimate sense of personal friendliness.

In the larger cities this wholesome tendency is still more in evidence. The small, exclusive circles composed of people possessing as nearly as possible the same degree of skin coloration, have been expanding, not only in their composition but also as regards their activities. A typical product of the new spirit is the club "Atenas" in the city of Havana. This is an organization which comprises in its active membership men and women of all shades of the colored race and counts as honorary members many white persons of the highest distinction.

"Atenas" is, as its name implies, a cultural center for the colored people of Cuba. Its activities are social in the fullest sense of the word. Its club rooms afford not only recreation and entertainment in the limited manner characteristic of such institutions, but also are opened for lectures, concerts and other manifestations of intellectual activity. With these efforts and through the medium of its monthly illustrated magazine, "Atenas" reveals to the colored people their own possibilities when they are willing to co-operate for their common welfare. At the same time, without making abstract and objective demands for political and other rights or advantages, it exerts a powerful influence in securing the respect and consideration of the best elements of white people.

Not with a sense of condescension, but with a feeling of ease and genuine appreciation of the opportunity to meet people of a different group but of their own intellectual and moral level, white friends attend, on invitation, the entertainments of "Atenas." Not long ago the club held a brilliant

reception in honor of a distinguished Cuban writer and generous friend of the colored race—a lady
who frequently visits this country, where she enjoys a large acquaintance. This reception was at
tended by many persons of the highest standing in
public affairs and in the various spheres of the
arts.

Occasions such as this mark the beginning of a
new epoch in the relations of white and colored
people in Cuba. In that Island, as in the rest of
the Latin countries, there is nothing extraordinary
in the meeting of people of pure European lineage
with persons of mixed race at private or public
gatherings. But in such cases the mixed people are
admitted not only as a necessary recognition of
their standing in the community, but because of
their partly European origin. The genuineness of
their welcome depends on the extent of their physical affinity to the white people, which they themselves always seek to regard as complete.

On the other hand, "Atenas" represents the effort of people who find in their non-European ancestry the principal motive for contact and co-operation. The fair mulatto is no longer ashamed of
his African blood. The pure black man is no longer restricted to the society of people of his own col-

or, for uniformity of complexion has ceased to be the indispensable basis for the constitution of a race or people. The white friends, and those who are not friends of "Atenas" can now see the possibility of the parallel development and neighborly existence of two groups of people, each respecting the other as well as itself, without a thought of the absorption or asphyxiation of one by the other.

The influence of this club is making itself felt throughout the Island of Cuba, and similar organizations are springing up in the smaller cities of the various Provinces. Ultimately, the colored people, by suppressing their own prejudices and showing that they can develop worthwhile institutions of their own, will achieve the equality which they could not obtain by force.

THE LIMITATIONS OF AMERICAN DEMOCRACY.

THE United States is unquestionably a democratic country, if by democracy is meant the
frankness of manner and simplicity of living of
its people. But the democracy of the United States
is not comprehensive of all the people; its application is limited to specific groups of the population,
characterized by affinity or identity of ethnic origin, of religion, of language, of customs. The spirit of tolerance and mutual respect among the members of one group is converted into a feeling of disrespect and hostility when applied to members of
another group. The play of these hostile forces
one upon the other serves as a restraining influence upon them all and produces as regards most of
them an external atmosphere of harmony and at
times, or cordiality. But this system of democracy
has not yet been extended to include white and colored people. Between these two major groups there
still remains in all its strength and inflexibility the
dividing line which separates autocracy and privilege from dependency and exploitation.

Throughout the civilized world the United States
is regarded as the symbol of democracy. This
opinion is well founded if we consider the guiding
principles of the political institutions of the country, the examples of men of humble birth who

have risen to the highest station in the various activities of the nation and in the opinion of its people. But as compared with the France that destroyed the Bastille and proclaimed the Rights of Man, the France that accords those rights to the black man as to all others, the country of Roosevelt is superior to the land of Victor Hugo only if the superficial is more important than the fundamental in the structure of a democratic people. A real democracy must be built up on the principles of equity summarized by Jose Marti in his campaign for the Independence of Cuba, "a Republic cordial with all and for all. " Such a nation was what the great restorer of the American Nation had in mind when he expressed the hope that the government and people of this country would, like himself, be animated and inspired "with justice to all, with malice toward none."

The people and the public powers of the United States have fallen far short of the ideal of Lincoln, not only in the relations of the various groups of the population, but especially as regards the attitude of the white man toward the black man. Democracy may subsist without intimate fellowship among those who share it, but it ceases to be real when one section of the people abuse their pow-

er in denying to members of a weaker section the
most elementary claims of justice. So long as there
exists a popular tendency among the white people
of the United States to commit crime under pre-
text of punishing the perpetrators of other crimes;
so long as the responsible and thinking elements of
the population, including the executive and legis-
lative powers, do not take steps for the effective
suppression of Lynch Law, the United States will
not have earned the place which, in many other
respects, it so richly deserves, among the leading
forces of human progress.

A great democracy cannot be constituted merely by the declaration of certain fundamental principles which are thereafter violated with impunity.
It is not enough for the basic law of the land to
set forth the equality of citizens, if in practice the
rights accruing therefrom are systematically and
persistently abridged or denied to certain citizens.
Democracy can hardly be said to have progressed
when women are granted the right of suffrage,
while this right is openly and admittedly taken
from men to whom it had been granted because
they had made themselves entitled to it.

A nation that deprives its own citizens of their
rights is not likely to have much genuine respect

for the rights of other nations. A great democracy must not only be a democracy at heart for and to all those whom it comprises, but it must apply the same principles in its relations with other nations. A strong democratic state must respect and seek to preserve rather than to destroy the liberty of weaker peoples. No matter what is said to the contrary, and there is much truth that may be said, the United States of America have by no means lived up to their professed abhorrence of autocracy and aggressive imperialism in their international affairs.

Nations which possess great material resources and materialized wealth do not tend to be truly democratic. As with wealthy individuals, their economic power is accompanied with a proportional haughtiness and pride and with progressively clearer expressions of autocracy. The United States is at present the wealthiest country in the world. Consequently, it is the most autocratic country, despite the existence, in some quarters, of a current of opinion which is as yet too weak to make itself felt to any appreciable extent. May the tide grow until the democracy of the United States embraces all its citizens in the application of equal justice before the law and in the mind of the people, upon whose will depends the enforcement of the law.

DEMOCRACY IN SPANISH AMERICA.

IN Spanish America, although his family history and his own position in the community may bring to a man a greater measure of respect and consideration for his person than would be the case in the United States, and class and individual distinctions are perhaps more marked in the former colonies of aristocratic Spain than in the republican descendant of England, yet it cannot be said with truth, as it often is affirmed on insufficient and misinterpreted evidence, that the political institutions of Latin America are essentially autocratic. If for no other reason the Spanish American countries are democratic because they are poor in realized wealth and are dependent on foreign capital to develop their economic resources; and as it is difficult for a moneyed country to be democratic, so is it easy and necessary for economically dependent countries to be democratic.

The Latin American peoples are essentially and passionately democratic in all things outside of their homes and personal relationships, for their economic development has not absorbed their attention. They have had time to keep alive the memories of their heroic struggles against autocracy and to foster the cult of Liberty. In all those countries the constitution, the whole theory of government, is democratic with an all inclusive democracy, which the people are always ready and determined to maintain unabridged. Contrary to the accepted opinion in other countries, the frequent revolutions in some of the Latin American countries are not necessarily harmful, for while they may temporarily interfere with the economic activity, they tend to ensure the political and moral integrity of the nation.

With rare exceptions, revolutions are not started to promote, but rather to counteract, personal ambitions. The attempt to overthrow a government is seldom inspired in the slightest degree by selfish motives, but rather by the determination to restore to the people the rights of which they are being progressively deprived by men who, having got into power by lawful means and in obedience to the public will, have failed to resist the temptation to extend their powers or the duration of office, sometimes for their personal advantage, sometimes in the sincere belief that they are the best and only qualified to manage the affairs of the state, but always obeying the dictate of unbridled egoism.

A typical illustration of the motive factors in a Latin American revolution is the following. A political party has secured the election of its candidate for president, by peaceful means and in accordance with constitutional procedure. When his term is drawing to a close, the president aspires to re-election, which, in the Latin American countries, is regarded as a principle of autocracy and is prohibited either by the letter of the law or the spirit of the people. But the retiring president and his associates or advisers avail themselves of the whole machinery of the government, including the army as a last resort, to coerce the people and prevent a free election. The leaders of the opposition are imprisoned; newspapers which venture to criticize the government are suppressed; the constitutional guaranties of the liberty of the citizens are suspended; and the president is re-elected.

This is a situation which many a Latin American country has been called upon to face. The ultimate remedy, no doubt, is education or occupation, not by alien authorities, but of the mind and hand of the native masses. Meantime, must an outraged people bow in supine resignation to the will of the usurper? Not while virile men are free and determined to remain free, as were the men who seeped their British tea in Boston Harbor.

Unfortunately, the impression prevails in the United States that revolutions are necessarily and invariably wrong and that the governments at which they are aimed are always right. Having assumed the role of big brother to the contentious small boys or creeping infants to the South, the Great Republic of North America has of recent years declared war on revolution by imposing on offending countries the penalty of non-recognition of a government empowered by revolution or, when practicable, by itself directly assuming the succession of the government which has been overthrown. Revolutions have lately been on the decrease in Latin America, but autocracy, native or foreign, has had proportionately more opportunity to destroy the results of a century of struggle for the maintenance of democratic government, in theory and practice.

An intelligent and helpful interest on the part of the United States with regard to the political affairs of the Latin American countries would not be based on the policy at present pursued by the Washington government. The government and people of the United States must understand that revolution is not an unmixed evil, and that every such occurrence must be judged impartially and with a full knowledge of the facts by any foreign power which proposes to further, and not to hinder, the progress of democracy in the Latin American countries.

WOMAN IN THE TWO AMERICAS.

FROM earliest childhood the Anglo-American woman enjoys a freedom of expression unknown to her Spanish-American sister. In the United States, the education of women, while it aims to conserve feminine charm and idealism, allows the fullest opportunity for the development and utilization of the talents of women in the material, practical spheres of life. The woman of the United States appreciates the spiritual value of familiarity with the plays of Shakespeare and the music of Verdi, but she also appreciates the value of the dollar which she has earned with her own brain and hand. She can discuss the subtleties of philosophy and religion while she plies her knitting in the subway. With her sex the world over, she shares the ideals of home and family, but she realizes that in order to have an ideal home and family, she must be willing and prepared when called upon to assume responsibilities which, in other countries, are borne exclusively and often imperfectly by men.

Trained to a life of activity, the American woman, on the completion of her education, ceases to be an economic burden on her parents. When she marries, her actual or potential contribution to the maintenance of the home places her in a position of equality with her husband. She is the partner and associate of the master of the household, rather than his mistress or slave. She is the companion whose counsel is sought and welcomed, not the dependent who obeys and dares not speak. Maintaining and asserting her personality no less in the home than in the office, the studio or the factory, she is a positive factor in the progress of her country.

Entirely different is the position of woman in Spanish America. Brought up in an atmosphere of seclusion and mysticism, the women of the higher classes usually begin their education with the study of Christian doctrine, with special emphasis on the lives of the saints, and end it with a course in languages and piano playing, at which many of them become expert. The women of the poorer classes, unable to attend the convent, imbibe as much as they can of feminine ideals or ideal femininity from their more favored sisters. Among rich and poor alike, the paramount service and duty of woman to society is to become as early as possible an obedient wife and as often as possible thereafter a fond and solicitous mother.

Without discarding these ideals, within recent years the Spanish American woman has been enjoying greater personal liberty and wider opportunity for the development of her abilities. In

many of the Latin countries, women now attend
the universities and professional schools on the
same terms as men. Before marriage they occupy
clerical positions and practise professions hitherto the exclusive perquisite of men. After marry-
ing, they utilize their training to help their hus-
bands maintain and increase the conjugal estate.
If they have wealth and leisure, their social and
altruistic activities no longer center exclusively
about the church, but extend to the more general
questions of public interest.

This change in the position of woman in Latin
America is, of course, slow and, in some countries, hardly appreciable. The modern woman
meets with much opposition, not only from the
men, but from within the ranks of her own sex.
It cannot be denied, however, that the most progressive countries are those which, without per-
mitting woman to participate actively in the affairs of the State, at least do not unduly hamper
her in the development and exercise of her talents
wherever she can unquestionably exert a benefi-
cent influence on the community. The new woman
in South America is largely a product of the increasing contact between that region and North
America. She is one product of definite, indis-
putable value, and her growing popularity can
never be seriously affected by competition.

SECTS AND SECRET SOCIETIES.

TO the foreign sojourner in the United States,
one of the most striking peculiarities of the
people of this country is the multiplicity of religious sects and secret societies. Although, as previous-
ly stated, the observations of the writer of these
notes have been in large measure confined to the
colored people, it is quite true that, in the matter
of secret societies as in the other characteristics
of their civilization, the colored people merely re-
flect the habits and customs of their white countrymen.

The writer's earliest impression of the freedom
of worship in the United States was produced by
the spectacle of the members of a sect marching
through the streets of Harlem to or from their
temple, two abreast, each carrying a copy of their
prayer-book, all dressed alike in flowing blue
robes, the masculine element being particularly
distinguished by wearing the hair and beard as
long as nature allows. On inquiry as to the identity of these remarkable persons, no definite in-
formation could be obtained; according to some
informers, the gentlemen and ladies of the Sacred
Order of the Blue Gown are black Jews who, like
their white co-religionists, manage to keep alive
their customs in a land of absolute liberty and

limited democracy; others say that they are disciples of the spiritualist Allan Kardeck.

Whatever may be the faith that moves these "black Jews," the interesting feature about them is that they are able to go about peacefully in the streets of New York and in their blue robes. In a South American country, if they were not molested by police agents detailed constantly to investigate their rites, they surely would be forced to disband if they did not want to convert their procession into a free circus. But an exhibition that would draw out the whole population of a South American town is so commonplace that it hardly arrests a glance in New York.

Perhaps in no other country, civilized or savage, are there so many secret organizations as in the United States, and certainly there is none where secrecy is so ostentatious. Hedge about with mystery the most significant acts and you have at once the nucleus of an association for some glorious object. But be sure to give half the secret away by displaying in public, in the summer or at other suitable times, the insignia of the order. The American secret society is, like the secret police, always ready to lose its secrecy by showing a button or badge.

Many of the organizations of this character in the United States are to be found in Europe and in Latin America, but not on the streets. The Masons, the Odd Fellows, the Knights of Columbus, the Shriners in the United States are so overburdened with their secrets that they share them periodically with the public by parading in their regalia. One society calls attention to its secrecy by allowing its members to display an emblem representing in its upper portion a sort of gong and in the lower part the head and antlers of a deer.

The type of a really secret society is probably best represented by the Ku Klux Klan, but even this organization enfolds most of its secrecy in the white sheet which its members wear in their public performances. The activity of this society is largely confined to the southern states and consists, besides the parades, of the exploitation of already thoroughly established and recognized prejudices of color and religion. The Ku Klux Klan has been accused, apparently with ample foundation, of perpetrating, under cover of the white sheets, the most barbarous and inhuman acts not only against colored people, but also against the other objects of the organization's displeasure. As the members of this society never reveal to out-

siders their connection with it, not even by showing their faces when on parade or when torturing
a victim, the secrecy of the society is so complete
that it has been impossible to suppress the organization or to discover and bring to justice those
of its members who may have been guilty of deeds
unworthy of civilized men.

Happily, the activities of the other secret societies, as regards the general public, are usually
limited to the display of their regalia. With rare
exceptions, they do not seek to exercise any collective influence on general social and political questions. They do not undertake to regulate the private conduct, either of outsiders or of their own
members. The American secret society merely re-
sponds to the demand of normal human beings for
fellowship and friendship, and the desire to pene-
trate the specious mysteries of a fraternal organization furnishes the occasion for contacts and associations which would otherwise be difficult of
realization among a people who are by training
reserved and individualistic.